Future Perfect

A Play

Emily Thwaite and Bill Sanderson

A Samuel French Acting Edition

SAMUEL FRENCH

FOUNDED 1830

SAMUELFRENCH-LONDON.CO.UK
SAMUELFRENCH.COM

FOR AMATEUR PRODUCTION ENQUIRIES

UNITED KINGDOM AND WORLD
EXCLUDING NORTH AMERICA
plays@SamuelFrench-London.co.uk
020 7255 4302/01

Each title is subject to availability from Samuel French,

depending upon country of performance.

FUTURE PERFECT

First performed, as *The Edge*, at The Town Hall, Wotton-under-Edge, Gloucestershire, on 8th August, 1998, with the following cast:

Scene Announcer	Roland McNulty
Orion	Barney Wakefield
Cassiopeia	Jane Randell
Chaos	Felix Harkness
Millie	Angharad Jonathan
Lennie	Will Sanderson-Thwaite
Em	Meg Randell
Perry	Jack Sanderson-Thwaite
Dawes	Alex Rigg
Charley	Hetty Horton
Pete	Andrew Perrett
First Bully	Kate Randell
Second Bully	Matthew Fowles
Bob Villum	Emily Barber
Mack E. Avelli	Steven Dexter
Ginger	Anna Pasco
Spotty	Josie Ward
Tommy	Maisie Sanderson-Thwaite
Snuffly	Katherine Barber
Baskerville	Roland McNulty
Barmen	Barney Wakefield, Ted Brandt, Phil Dodd
Farmers	Kirk Line, Sam Barber, Matthew Fowles, Phil Dodd
Acrobats	Kirk Line, Kate Randell

Dancers   Jack Sanderson-Thwaite, Alex Rigg,
Jane Randell, Barney Wakefield, Kate Randell,
Kirk Line, Maisie Sanderson-Thwaite, Josie Ward,
Anna Pasco, Katherine Barber, Kate Pasco, Emily
Barber, Steven Dexter, Sam Barber, Phil Dodd
Robots   Members of the cast
Machines   Members of the cast
Fairground Stallholders   Kirk Line,
Maisie Sanderson-Thwaite,
Kate Pasco, Sam Barber
Fire-eater   Meg Randell
Snake-charmer   Ted Brandt
Snake   Matthew Fowles

Lighting by **Wes McNulty**, **Felix Harkness**

CHARACTERS
(up to 70 children)

Scene Announcer, brings a board on bearing the name of the scene, before each scene

Orion, king of the overworld
Cassiopeia, queen of the overworld
Chaos, an evil spirit of the overworld
Large puppets (taller than life-size), designed to be operated by children and capable of being free-standing so the children operating them can rest

Millie, their daughter
Lennie, their son
Em, their youngest child

Perry*, go-between and master of ceremonies
Dawes*, go-between and master of ceremonies
Dressed as fairground barkers, with straw boater, bow tie, stripey waist-coat, bright braces, white trousers, etc.
*Choose names of local worthies

Charley, a local child (girl)
Pete, a local child (boy)
First Bully, a local child (girl)
Second Bully, a local child (boy)

Bob Villum, a villain, dressed in a "sharp" suit (female)
Mack E. Avelli, a villain, dressed in "sharp" suit (male)

Ginger, a guinea pig
Spotty, a puppy
Tommy, a cat
Snuffly, a rabbit
Baskerville,** a lizard

**appears first as a small hand puppet, then a child in similar costume

6 Barmen/women
4 Farmers
Acrobats
Dancers
Robots, children in robot costumes, loose enough to allow them to dance
Machines, children in metallic-looking costumes, not too restrictive. Not covering heads: black veils over faces, instead
Fairground Stallholders
Snake-charmer and Snake

Musicians, playing violins, tambourines, drums, accordion/concertina, piano/keyboard, recorders/tin whistles, cymbals, flexible boards and other percussion for sound effects

Acknowledgement

The extract from the poem *Wotton Walks* is reprinted by permission of the poet, U.A. Fanthorpe.

Music

The specially composed music by Phil Andrews for this play is available on hire from Samuel French Ltd. A fee is payable for the use of this music in conjunction with performances of the play.

Please read the notice supplied by the Performing Right Society on page xii if any other copyright music is used in connection with this play

AUTHORS' NOTES

Our play, *Future Perfect*, imagines a future where a town which is "Under the Edge" has a connection with a world above it: "Over the Edge". The Edge is a flexible line between the two worlds.

We first staged it in the summer of 1998, when our three children and 22 of their friends (ages ranging from 7 to 14) worked on it, for a week, with us. We had not scripted it before this time, but arrived at the beginning of the week, having only prepared a synopsis of each scene. We had met with all the children in the spring, when we discussed ideas for the play, and discovered what type of character each child wanted to play.

During the summer week, the children improvised each scene, arriving at words that felt appropriate for their character and situation. So, many of these words that you will read, and perform, are the children's own. A list of the original cast appears on page iii.

Our home town is Wotton-under-Edge in Gloucestershire. The poem that opens the prologue is taken from *Wotton Walks*, by U. A. Fanthorpe, the perfect choice for our town:

> Enter this web
> Spun by dead and living round Wotton.
> Remember lovers keeping trysts
> At special stiles, remember
> Gipsies stealing down green lanes,
> And the reflective fellows
> Who watched and thought by bridges
> Over small streams. Attend also
> To the punctually returning
> Tree, flower, bird, since what you see
> Is as new as it's old.
> Finally,
> Come back satisfied, please, at peace,
> To where Wotton pleats herself on her shelves
> Above the vale, under the edge.

For your own town, of course, you can choose a poem that feels right for your part of the country, or you could even write your own. In addition, at the end of the play, we chose to recite *The Trees*, a beautiful poem by Philip Larkin, which seemed really appropriate.

We would also like to acknowledge Phil Andrews and Simon McNulty, who composed and performed the music for our songs, and provided some of the incidental music.

As the play involves two worlds with a permeable border, the staging should reflect this. Ideally, the space available for *Future Perfect* will include a stage (referred to here as *top stage*), with side-steps to the floor; and a semi-circular floor space (referred to here as *lower stage*), around which the audience can be seated (referred to here as *the house*). A large stage block, or group of smaller blocks, remains on the lower stage, DC, throughout the play.

Well, we hope you all enjoy putting on your own production of this play. There should be plenty of scope for you to adapt it, so that you feel that it is about your own home.

Bill Sanderson and Emily Thwaite

FUTURE PERFECT

PROLOGUE

Lights: the top and lower stages are dark

Voices off (including Orion and Cassiopeia), recite a poem about two worlds meeting. (This could be written by the children about your town)

Perry and Dawes enter from the back of the house

Perry I hear our master Orion.
Dawes And our mistress Cassiopeia calls us.

Perry and Dawes go up the steps to the side of top stage and wait off

SCENE 1

Over the Edge—Arrival

Music: formal/baroque theme (e.g. Purcell, Monteverdi), played by the school orchestra/music group

Lights: top stage, blue gels, pool of moonlight; lower stage, dark; house lights, down

Orion and Cassiopeia enter from opposite sides of the top stage, each holding a large flower. Their children, Millie and Lennie, walk, hidden, behind them. Millie is behind Orion and Lennie behind Cassiopeia

They move as if stepping a formal dance:
> *4 side steps into the middle of the top stage, facing the audience*
> *They acknowledge each other*
> *Millie and Lennie kneel down behind Orion and Cassiopeia*
> *Orion and Cassiopeia take a large step each to the sides, revealing Millie and Lennie*
> *Orion and Cassiopeia give the flowers to the children—Orion to Millie, Cassiopeia to Lennie*

Millie and Lennie stand up, cross behind/in front of each other, spin round and present their parents with the flowers—Millie to Cassiopeia, Lennie to Orion
Millie and Lennie hold out hands to each other and pull themselves in to stand next to each other again

During the following, one of the two go-betweens, Perry, comes down the stage steps to the lower stage, and stands at the side

Millie and Lennie skip to the front of the stage (in a choreographed routine, if wanted), jump forward and then sit, at the same time, on the edge of the stage, legs dangling over

Perry (*talking to himself*) Oh, they've turned up then. Quite a lot really. They look a bit rough round the edges, but they'll do. I'd better make a start. (*He walks* C *of the lower stage, straightens his tie, consults a long piece of paper, frowns and takes a deep breath. Then, slowly at first, getting faster:*)
My lords, ladies and gentlemen…
boys and girls, aunts in curls, uncles, cousins, sometimes dozens,
grannies, granddads, nanas and granpas,
cats, dogs, even frogs,
hamsters, gangsters, merchant bankers,
friends, Romans and fellow country men…
(*he takes another deep breath, checking off on his fingers*)
visitors to the town, country walkers,
hangers-on and endless talkers,
just popped out to buy a paper, must go now, I'll see you later,
passing clouds, shoppers, boppers,
two small girls on red spacehoppers…
coach parties, hale and hearties, sophisticates and
(*pointedly at the front row/headteacher*) gormless gawkers.

He pauses, looks round at the audience and smiles

During the following, Dawes enters backwards and will collide with his mate

Perry (*to the audience*) Now, have I missed anyone out? No? All right now? … Sorry, I can't hear you.

He elicits a loud "Yes" from the audience

Good. Welcome to the wonderful Wotton [*substitute the name of your*

town/area, with an enthusiastic alliterative adjective in front of it] Fair.
There's a wonderful evening in store for you all, you'll see much more than
you ever imagined existed. Wotton is an unusual place, strange things
happen here, peculiar things, just when you least expect them.

Dawes bumps into Perry. They both get a fright

Oh, you've finally arrived, then. What happened to you?
Dawes I forgot something.
Perry What did you forget?
Dawes I forgot what time it was…
Perry Now where was I? Oh yes, Wotton is unusual.
Dawes (*echoing with agreement and emphasis*) Mmm. Unusual.
Perry Some might say peculiar.
Dawes Mmm. Peculiar.
Perry Wotton holds a very special position. It connects two worlds. It is on
  the edge, you might say.
Dawes The edge…
Perry Anyway, you'll see. Now, we introduce to you, for your pleasure and
  entertainment, the wonderful Wotton Fair. Don't worry, we'll stick around
  and help you out if it all gets too hard to follow.

*Perry and Dawes exit, greeting the Acrobats, Musicians, Stallholders and
the Scene Announcer as they go*

SCENE 2

Under the Edge—The Fairground

*Music: country dancing tunes, played by violin, tambourine, drums, accordion/
concertina*

*Lights: top stage, blue gels; lower stage, bright with spot C; house lights,
down*

*Four booths for fairground games (coconut shy, hook-a-duck, blow football
and fire breathing: symbolising earth, water, air and fire) are erected*

*Acrobats open the proceedings, tumbling/cartwheeling/flipping from various
directions, in turn*

*Strolling Musicians then appear and eventually take up positions to accompany
country/maypole dancing*

Dancers enter (however many groups there is space for) and dances begin— one after the other, or the same one in unison: traditional tune and dance, or specially composed and choreographed

Stallholders then start setting up their stalls, putting out prizes, etc.

People enter, in groups, twos and threes, looking round the Fair. Small children are dodging through the crowd

The spotlight focuses on one stall at a time, with appropriate things said and done at each

[1] Coconut shy

Stallholder 1 Step right up, knock it down, take it home, hard as you like.

A very confident boy plays, misses every time

[2] Blow football

Stallholder 2 Come on, play the game, win the cup.

Friends who haven't seen each other for ages meet and play enthusiastically

[3] Hook a duck

Stallholder 3 Try your luck and hook a duck.

Excited players concentrate, winners clutch their prizes proudly

[4] Fire eater

Stallholder 4 Step up and see the woman who breathes fire—don't step too close, you'll lose your eyebrows.

Astonished people step back and gasp in awe. A little child is frightened, comforted by father

Other comments about the stalls can be improvised, but make sure that each activity has a distinct time in focus

A Snake Charmer reveals himself and performs a snake-charming act, playing a tin whistle or recorder. The Snake can be played by a small child, rising out of a large round basket in time to the music. A fairground audience sits in a semi-circle on the floor round the charmer and snake. At the end of his act, a lizard, Baskerville, (a puppet operated by the Snake Charmer) appears. He watches and listens attentively to the following episode

Charley and Pete appear amongst the stalls

Charley is bored and unimpressed by the fair and won't spend her money on anything. Pete is excited by it all, and tries to persuade Charley to enjoy herself and have a go on something

Two Bullies appear

They spot Charley and Pete and stalk them through the crowd. They accost them—misleading taps on shoulder, shoves, etc.—and force them to hand over their money. Pete is dejected

Charley runs off

The bullies have an argument about sharing the money—the girl wins and, running off, tells her "mate" he'll only get a share, "in your dreams"

All freeze

SCENE 3

Over the Edge—The Argument

Music: Monteverdi/Over the Edge theme; later, storm sound effects—made by children with cymbals, flexible board, drums, etc.

Lights: top stage, blue flashes of lightning; lower stage, red storm lightning

Orion and Cassiopeia are on stage with Millie and Lennie still sitting on the edge

Cassiopeia I think it's time our children went out to see the world.
Orion But they're too young.
Cassiopeia There's so much to see and experience out there.
Orion Our children are not ready, they're still ignorant of the way things work.
Cassiopeia That's why they need to go and find out for themselves.

Orion They should learn by studying first, to be prepared.
Cassiopeia Oh, you're so stuffy.
Orion I'm only thinking of them. I don't want them to get hurt.
Cassiopeia *You* don't want them to grow up. They're not babies any more.
Orion *You* don't want them cramping your style. You just want them out of the way.

Both characters are getting louder and more heated now. The storm sound effects start in the background, getting louder during the following but not so as to drown the words. Millie and Lennie sneak off during this, down to the lower stage, via the steps

Cassiopeia How dare you suggest that?
Orion But it's true. You're so selfish.
Cassiopeia Oh, you're impossible. Just let our children enjoy themselves for a change. We were young once, remember? Or have you grown too old and boring?
Orion Huh! You're irresponsible, that's what you are. The world is a dangerous place.
Cassiopeia Millie and Lennie can look after themselves. They've got sense. Unlike you.
Orion You're the one who talks nonsense.
Cassiopeia Oh, I won't stand for this.

Orion and Cassiopeia both storm off, one to each side

The storm sound effects reach a climax

Scene 4

Under the Edge—The Storm

Music: storm sound effects—gradually dying away to steady rain (children with "rain-maker" tubes)

Lights: top stage, occasional blue flashes of lightning; lower stage, red/blue glow

As the rain gets stronger, the Stallholders are packing up, putting away the prizes and equipment. The stalls are then cleared away DL *and* DR

Two children create a flood (long blue material) flapping/rushing in front of the central block

Animals appear on the block (which now represents an island in the middle of the flood): Guinea pig burbling, Puppy whimpering, Cat mewing, Rabbit twitching

Pete enters in search of his friend Charley. He goes off calling her

Charley enters (from a different direction), notices the animals and swims to the island to try to help them, but is then stuck herself

She tries her best to comfort the animals

Charley Don't worry; someone will rescue us; you'll soon be home and dry again; the storm can't go on for ever; keep making your noises, they're bound to hear you.

Other children, offstage, could make the animal sounds as well, to amplify the animals on stage—this should probably be orchestrated, so it's not all at once

Millie and Lennie enter, looking around eagerly

The animals are quieter at this point

Pete returns and mistakes Millie for Charley

Pete Oh, I thought you were my friend Charley. I've lost her. I must find her quickly, especially in this weather.

The three children introduce themselves to each other. Lennie then hears the animals crying and notices Charley. The rabbit points out (with her/his ear) some wood in a pile. She/he twitches her/his nose indicating that it could be used for rescuing them—Lennie obviously understands this language, and he gets Pete and Millie to help him build a bridge across the swollen stream. Meanwhile, Charley is alternately shouting complaints and encouragement

Charley Hurry up, it's freezing over here. Careful you don't get stuck.

Charley and the animals eventually cross to safety and the bridge is then shaken to bits by fast water

Millie and Lennie make friends with Pete and Charley, and they arrange to meet the following day

Pete Where shall we meet?

Pete and Charley list local landmarks (about four or five), none of which Millie and Lennie recognize

Pete
Charley } (*together*) Don't you know anywhere?

They decide to meet here, where they are now

Pete and Charley exit

The animals come up to Lennie and he realizes he can understand them. He learns their names: Tommy (cat), Spotty (dog), Snuffly (rabbit), Ginger (guinea-pig). He asks the animals to tell Millie what they're called. The animals do this

Lennie Did you hear their names?
Millie All I heard was miaowing, barking, squeaking … oh, and snuffling.

Both Lennie and Millie are impressed by the discovery of Lennie's power. The animals suggest, to Lennie, a place where the children can spend the night

They all exit

SCENE 5

Under the Edge—The Pitch in the Pub

Music: jolly music while pub bars are being set up; pub background noise, chatting, clinking, later, perhaps made off or pre-recorded on a tape; song, What a Life It'll Be to "Cockney" singalong piano music; robotic sounds for robot dance at the end

Lights: top stage, dark; lower stage, bright interior

Six Barmen/women enter

They set up three bars in front of the stage. (Use three of the fairground stalls, turning them round so surfaces are available to customers for drinks.) They put out chairs in the body of the pub—lower stage area. They clean glasses, put out beer mats/cloths etc. Two of them set out a cloth and food on one of the side-bars, and chairs

Perry and Dawes enter and sit here, eating and drinking quietly: they seem to be regulars, given special service. Two more Barmen/women then reveal the name of the pub (covered over, on the c bar)—choose a local name from your area

Barman/woman All right, Jim/Jo, open up.

Jim/Jo goes over to let in the customers

Background noise starts, building up gradually. A darts game sets up (several children, dressed as farmers, with hats, waistcoats/fleeces, boots) centrally. Other farmers play dominoes at a group of chairs at the side

After a few moments, for the scene to register, Bob Villum and Mack E. Avelli enter, carrying clipboards and pens

The background noise stops abruptly

Everyone in the pub turns to look at them, registering that they are newcomers/intruders. Bob and Mack move the domino players out of their seats. They plot thickly for a while

Mack They're a pushover this lot.
Bob I'll have them eating out of my hand, just watch me.
Mack I'll back you up.

Bob gets up on to a chair to do her pitch

Bob Ladies and gentlemen, listen up. You don't know me, but I've been watching you. This is a wonderful town, and you all seem really nice people. But you have a very hard life, many of you, wouldn't you agree?

The farmers look at each other, a bit surprised but acquiescent—Bob then gives examples of how hard the farming life is

You don't want to get up in the cold and dark to milk the cows, do you? You don't want to break your back forking hay into the loft, surely? You don't want to bake in the sun getting the harvest in before it rains? Why not go for the easy life? Sign up with me and your lives will be transformed. No more work at all. I've got it sorted. Automation. That's the word. Fancy word. Simple idea. Let machines take the strain, carry the grief, suffer the sweat.

Mack looks at Bob, perplexed. Bob realizes she's getting carried away

What I'm telling you is this: everything can be done at the touch of a button. And I can arrange it. (*She waits for the farmers' reactions*)

Some of them are not too sure at first and ask awkward questions—she has an answer for everything. Mack pretends to be won over, and once he signs up, the rest follow suit

Farmer (*enthusiastically, loudly*) What a life it'll be.

Music for the song. The whole pub ends up singing it, swinging and rocking in time. During the song Bob and Mack go round the front row of the audience, getting them to sign a contract to join their scheme

All   I don't know whether or not I'll be
Happy if I win the lottery
But I'd take a chance and risk a bit of strife
You may think it's pretty flirty
To bet on the two-thirty
When I've never ever seen a horse race in my life

But I'm sick of nine to fiving
It's not living, it's surviving
And I never get a chance to see my wife!

But these Bob and Mack blokes promise us
That they'll change it all and bring the buzz
Of automated farming to our life
No more mucking out at daybreak or
Traipsing cow muck on the kitchen floor
Or picking prickles from my bottom with a knife!

The machines will do it for us
In a labour-saving chorus
And they will even make me smell nice for my wife.

What a life it'll be
In bed till three
And never lift a finger any more.

What a life it'll be
For little old me
I'll stay up late and watch the final score!

What a life it'll be

> Sleeping under a tree
> And drinking pints of lager when I wake.
>
> What a life it'll be
> Always out on a spree
> And eating lots of lovely cream cake.

Bob (*to everyone*) Do you want to meet our robot helpers?

Mack leads the robots on in a robotic dance. (Work out a simple routine, precise and impersonal)

All exit

SCENE 6

Under the Edge—The Powers are Revealed

Lights: top stage, dark; lower stage, bright exterior

Millie and Lennie are sitting down

Charley and Pete enter talking

Charley I wonder if they're here yet.

They all then notice each other

Charley
Pete } (*together*) Do you want to play a game?
Millie
Lennie } (*together*) OK.
Charley What shall we play?
Pete Hopscotch.
Millie
Lennie } (*together*) What's that?

Charley and Pete teach them to play, Charley drawing out the grid, Pete talking. They thoroughly confuse Millie and Lennie. Charley calls the stone a stoof (use a local word), and Pete tells the rules too quickly. Charley gives a fast demonstration

Pete Do you want a go now, Millie?

*Millie looks very unsure but tries anyway. She places the stone on the
number 3*

No. You've got to throw it.

Millie picks it up and jumps

Charley (*shouting*) You didn't throw the stoof.
Millie (*screaming, in frustration*) STOP!

Charley and Pete freeze. Millie and Lennie wonder what Millie has done

Lennie (*to Charley and Pete*) Go back.

Charley and Pete start moving backwards as if in a tape rewinding

This is fun!
Millie We've got extra powers.

Charley is just about to pick up the stone, as if to start the demonstration again

STOP.

*Millie and Lennie put the stone behind Charley. Millie clicks her fingers to
make time start again. Charley looks in her hand for the stone. Millie and
Lennie point it out behind her*

Lennie It must have walked.
Pete (*astonished*) Stoofs don't walk!

Millie and Lennie smile at each other

The animals enter

They talk to Lennie US. *Charley, Pete and Millie sit on a rock (the stage block)*
DS. *Lennie translates the animals' talk for them. They are invited on a picnic*

Cat Don't forget to watch the road.
Rabbit And wash your hands before eating.
Charley (*to Millie*) How does Lennie know what they're saying?
Millie I'll tell you on the way.

The animals and children exit

The Bullies from the fairground enter

Bully 1 That was those kids.
Bully 2 Let's give them a big surprise when they get back.

They hide, one each side of the rock

Millie, Lennie, Charley and Pete come back, discussing the excellent picnic

Millie That casserole the rabbit made for us was the best.
Charley Wasn't the fruit cocktail yummy?
Lennie The guinea-pig tosses a mean pancake.
Pete And these sweets will just round it all off nicely.

The Bullies jump out on the children and take the sweets. They are about to eat them

Millie STOP.

The Bullies freeze

Millie tells Lennie to help her switch the sweets for mud and stones. Millie clicks her fingers. The Bullies are revolted by what they eventually taste

The Bullies run off, sworn on revenge

As the children walk off, they meet Perry and Dawes

Perry Well, you certainly dealt with them.
Dawes But watch out, even greater trouble is round the corner.
Perry Bob Villum and Mack E. Avelli are in town, with their nasty plans.

Millie and Lennie nod knowingly and look serious. Pete and Charley have never heard of those characters before, and look worried

SCENE 7

Over the Edge—Together Again

Music: Over the Edge theme

Lights: top stage, warm yellow, pools of light; lower stage, dark, but with Millie and Lennie visible

Millie and Lennie are sitting down, lower stage (on the block). They look upwards when the music starts, remembering their parents (but not seeing them)

Orion and Cassiopeia enter

Music continues quietly

Orion and Cassiopeia apologise to each other for their previous argument. They each blame themselves, and excuse themselves, and pledge never to start an argument again, praising each other's good temper, etc. etc. They each deny vehemently that it could be the other one's fault

Cassiopeia Oh, let's not start arguing again.

They are worried about their children Millie and Lennie

Orion They are Under the Edge now.
Cassiopeia Will they be safe?
Orion The people Under the Edge are ruining their world with all their machines and pollution.
Cassiopeia Will we ever see our children again?
Orion Oh, Millie and Lennie, how can we get you back?

Em appears from behind Orion and Cassiopeia and suggests that she could go to save her brother and sister

But Em, you are our only remaining child, our youngest.
Cassiopeia You have never been near that dangerous place.
Em But remember, because I am the youngest and have been with you constantly I will be able to keep the power of my home inside me. I can link the two worlds, Over the Edge and Under the Edge.
Cassiopeia Well, it seems as if this is our only hope.
Orion Take care, Em.
Em I will always be able to hear what you are thinking and you will hear me.

Em descends to Under the Edge, down the stage steps

SCENE 8

Under the Edge—The World gone Mad

Music: electronic techno—for rap and dance of the Combine Pillagers

Lights: top stage, dark; lower stage, harsh and bright

Four Farmers (from Scene 5, the pub) enter, along with other farmworkers

They begin working—a different activity in each quarter of the lower stage: e.g. choose from weeding, forking hay, digging, breaking stones, hoeing, sowing seeds. They wipe their brows periodically, and otherwise indicate the hard physical labour. (Possibly accompanied by taped background sound effects of birds, insects and summery countryside sounds)

Bob and Mack enter, carrying helmets (made from cardboard boxes perhaps) with coloured visors, tubes and aerials sticking out. They approach the first farmer

Bob You remember us, don't you? Well, we're here to keep our promises. Your life is going to be easier from now on.

The farmer looks expectant

Mack What are you waiting for? You've got to keep *your* part of the bargain too.
Bob Yes, hurry up, man. Hand over the cash.

Reluctantly, the farmer gives the money. Bob puts a helmet over his head, and helmets over the heads of the workers in his section

Farmer 1 (*exclaiming*) Oh, I can't believe this, there's not a weed in sight. Our work's done already.

Bob and Mack then go to the other farmers, take their money and put the helmets on

Mack A worthy exchange!

When all are helmeted, the background sounds fade to a sinister buzzing. In turn, the farmers exclaim at what they see through the helmets—i.e. transformed fields. They each say something appropriate to their previous tasks

Farmers   The trees are so heavy with fruit
                The hay has been stacked
                The wheat is ripe and golden

Bob and Mack's pièce de résistance *is getting the farmers to stand as if inside a car, two at the front and two at the back, and then believe that they're in a Rolls Royce with leather seats and fittings, shiny door handles, etc. Bob hands the farmer in the passenger seat a painted stone*

Bob Enjoy your trip, you deserve a break, and here's a delicious ice-cream to get you in the mood.

The farmer goes to lick the stone as the four "drive" off. Bob and Mack laugh wickedly

The new Machines arrive. The costumes echo the style of the helmets. Music heralds them, electronic techno. They enter through the audience, moving mechanically, dragging heavy black/silver/grey plastic sheets which they leave on the ground behind them—a concrete desert over the fields

When they are on the lower stage they get into groups, and start their aggressive rap, The Song of the Combine Pillagers, *accompanying themselves on metal and hard plastic pipes etc.*

Different groups of Machines, and individuals, should take different lines

Song of the Combine Pillagers

Pillagers We like noise and we like dust,
               We don't care for the National Trust.
               We are steel and we are flames,
               We destroy all country lanes,
               And no-one ever dares to stop the rot.
               We are looters with big hooters,
               And we never never miss a beauty spot.

Chorus   Swish, swish, crash, crash,
               Watch out, little baby, it's a combine!
               Thrash, thrash, clash, clash,
               Baby, better get right outta my way!

Pillagers We bring death and eco-doom,
               We've never entered Britain in Bloom.
               We love to spoil and live to pillage,

As we travel through each Cotswold [your county] village,
And spit out toxic gases in salute.
We're fantastic, we love plastic
And we never never miss a scenic route. .

Chorus   Swish, swish, crash, crash,
Watch out, little baby, it's a combine!
Thrash, thrash, clash, clash,
Baby, better get right outta my way!

Pillagers   Destroying, never gets annoying,
As we charge around the country in a spin.
Don't you mind it,
When you find it,
You'll be happy making such a lovely din.

We are dirty, we are grey,
We leave muck on the Cotswold [local name] Way
We're the best, don't need a rest,
As we knock the little birdies off their nest,
And we'll fill your pond with bedsteads in a trice.
We're disgusting, nature busting,
We're not only very naughty, we're not nice!

Chorus   Swish, swish, crash, crash,
Watch out, little baby, it's a combine!
Thrash, thrash, clash, clash,
Baby, better get right outta my way!

All exit

*Millie, Lennie, Charley and Pete enter and are horrified by what they see—
the concrete and filth/mess/dirt covering and spoiling the landscape.
Millie and Charley sit on the rock* C, *Lennie kneels* UL, *Pete stands* UR

Lennie Bob Villum and Mack E. Avelli did this.
Pete Why do they hate the countryside so much?

Em arrives R

*She goes straight over to Millie who greets her warmly. Millie introduces her
to Charley, and then to Pete. Lennie comes over*

Lennie But why have you come, Em? It's getting dangerous here.

Em That's why. Our parents are worried about you. I must keep the link
going between Over and Under. (*She stops talking and looks very serious,
staring straight ahead and concentrating hard*) Orion and Cassiopeia are
pleased you're both safe.

Charley and Pete look at each other in astonishment

But we must stop those villains. If we don't, the connection between our
two places will break for ever.
Millie Well, what are we waiting for? Let's go.
Em We must have a plan, though. Where's Bob's and Mack's base?
Charley I think it must be that new black dome.
Pete Covering what used to be Waterley Bottom [a local park/beauty spot].
Lennie There must be a central computer in there.
Millie Yes, to control those machines and makes the farmers see things that
don't exist. So let's go *now*.

Em leads them all off

SCENE 9

Under the Edge—Plan of Action

Music: suspense made by recorders etc.; later, melancholy piano song,
Don't Give Up Hope

Lights: top stage, dark; lower stage, dim, follow spot later

The Bullies enter and settle down to sleep beside the rock

The children creep in, led by Em, with Lennie at the back

*Em gets on the rock, the others kneel in front of her. In a stage whisper Em
explains the plan, e.g.:*

We'll sneak inside and head for the main computer…
What if it goes wrong?
We've got to try something. (*Etc.*)

They leave L

*The Bullies stand up and say they're going to tell Bob and Mack about the
children's plans, (getting their own back):*

Bullies We might get a reward.

The Bullies leave L

Bob and Mack enter R

They work various machines, levers, etc. Facing the audience, they gloat over how their plans are almost complete

The Bullies enter R *and tell Bob and Mack what they've overheard. Bob and Mack set a trap with the help of the Bullies. Bob tells Mack to switch off the lights*

In semi-darkness, Em, Millie, Charley, Pete and Lennie enter, in line— Lennie still at the back

When they're all in, Bob springs the trap. The Lights come on simultaneously. Em, Millie, Charley and Pete are trapped with helmets

Millie (*to Lennie*) RUN.

Lennie runs out L

All freeze

Black-out, during which all exit

Lennie enters, alone and dejected

Follow spot on Lennie. He is angry with himself for not doing more to help the others. He begins to sing Don't Give Up Hope (*possibly have a microphone waiting for him*), *sitting on the rock*

As Lennie sings, the animals come on to share the rock with him. They cuddle and comfort him. They join in with singing the chorus

Don't Give Up Hope

Lennie   Just now this world seems lonely and unfriendly
I can't imagine ever getting through
'Cos there is no-one else around to lend me
A hand, when going on seems hard to do.

Chorus   Don't give up hope

Don't let them win
Doubting voices come crowding in your mind.
Believe you'll cope
Come through again
Push back the shadows, leave the fears behind

Lennie   Under the Edge, I thought I'd find a way
To make sense of what it is I'm here to do
But now I'm scared, I'm really scared that my friends may
Be relying on my strength to see them through

Chorus   Don't give up hope
Don't lose the light
For darkness never lasts beyond the dawn
Don't give up hope
And you just might
Find the secret that's been kept since you were born.

Repeat Chorus Don't give up hope
Don't lose the light
For darkness never lasts beyond the dawn
Don't give up hope
And you just might
Find the secret that's been kept since you were born.

SCENE 10

Under the Edge—Deeper and Deeper

Music: wicked, scary

Lights: top stage, dark; lower stage, interior, night, spooky

Bob and Mack enter

They stand on the platform and gloat over their success, counting wads of notes

During the following, Chaos appears on the top stage, behind Bob and Mack, with a red spotlight on him

Bob We've really done well this week; we've made so much profit.

Mack We certainly conned those farmers, they're eating out of our hands.
Bob Think of all the holidays we can go on, the flash cars we can buy.
Mack The world is our oyster.
Chaos (*shouting*) STOP! (*He stretches his arm/claw out towards Bob*)

Bob turns round, as if gripped. Mack edges away and then he also freezes, mysteriously held in Chaos's power

(*Booming*) The world is MINE. You think you've done well? A handful of farmers is not enough. I want the countryside devastated. I want *everyone* under my control.

Bob and Mack quake and apologise

Bob We *do* understand.
Mack We *have* got those children for you.
Chaos Ah yes, those wretched children. It is not enough that they are captured. You must send them to me. I will deal with them once and for all. Remember, you get nothing until you have completed my task. Wotton [*your town*] is not enough. I want to rule Britain. I need to control THE WORLD.

Chaos exits

Over the Edge goes dark. Bob and Mack discuss their situation

Mack I wish we'd never got into this.
Bob We've got no choice now, we can't disobey him, we must finish his work.

Black-out, during which Bob and Mack exit

SCENE 11

Under the Edge—Everyone Can Help

Music: sound effects of earthquake and storm to be made by the audience; sound of thunderclap on tape would be good

Lights: top stage, dark; lower stage, interior, bright; house lights, up

Perry and Dawes enter, with a bag/box of percussion instruments and a lightning flash prop

Perry Hallo again.

He pauses for audience response

This time, sadly, I bring bad news. All of the children, except Lennie, have been captured…
Dawes But with a little help from you, the children could defeat those evil villains.
Perry Now, for this we are going to split the audience up in to three sections, a, b and c. You, (*he indicates all of stage right*), will be section a.
Dawes And you, (*he indicates all of stage left*) will be section b.
Perry And you, (*he picks out one person from the audience, possibly the headteacher*) will be section c. Now I want my section, section a, to be an earthquake. I've got something here that might help you. (*He hands out a percussion instrument*)

Perry interacts with the audience, e.g. if they start too soon, he says wearily "Not yet, wait for it. Let's have a little control here or it'll fall apart"

Now, when I say the word, you can start.
Dawes What word?
Perry Oh, yes, thank you, Dawes—we need to choose a password. Something appropriate that Lennie will be able to remember. Any ideas?

More interaction with the audience. If they suggest silly passwords, like "sausages", Perry could say, "I should have known better than to expect something sensible from you lot." Eventually, though, Perry shouldn't wait too long for suggestions. The performer needs to take charge, lead the proceedings

Did someone say *shake*? That'll do. So, let's try. Listen out for the word. Sh, sh, sugar. (*He looks exasperatedly at those who started by mistake*) Come on, keep up, please! *Shake*!

The audience should then shake their instruments, bang feet, roar etc. When the "earthquake" is over, Dawes speaks

Dawes Not much to beat then, section b. You can do far better than that. You are going to be wind and rain, so make plenty of swooshing, howling, pattering, wet and windy noises basically. We need a password too. Any suggestions? (*After a few audience suggestions, he decides on "storm"*) Let's practise. *Storm*!

The audience makes their noises

Perry Now, section c. You'll need this. (*He shows the audience the lightning flash, then hands it over*) It's a lightning bolt. When Lennie says *flash*…
Dawes You get up quickly and clean the kitchen floor!
Perry (*sarcastically*) Thank you, Dawes. As I was saying, when he says *flash* you point the bolt where he shows you.

They practise. First Perry mimes the action—total silence—then he invites section c to do likewise. This time an enormous thunderclap (tape) sounds when section c points the bolt

Now we'll go and find Lennie. Don't forget your parts.
Dawes We're relying on you.
Perry Listen out for those passwords.

SCENE 12

Under the Edge—The Rescue Begins

Music: suspense, trembling recorders

Lights: top stage, dark; lower stage, c spot on Lennie, moonlight, and follow spot

Lennie enters L, dejected and tired

He sits on the rock, facing UL

Baskerville appears in the distance R—the lizard puppet from the fairground scene (now a performer, dressed similarly to the puppet)

Lennie hears a noise and turns round to face the lizard. He moves backwards, fearful. Baskerville walks on to the lower stage. He moves forward to the rock

Baskerville (*loud and slow*) Do not be frightened!
Lennie Who are you?
Baskerville My name is Baskerville.

Lennie decides to let Baskerville in on the secret, telling him about his sisters' and friends' predicament

Lennie They're being held captive in the black dome, the headquarters of Bob Villum and Mack E. Avelli.

Baskerville (*thinking about this*) Hmm… (*Slowly*) I know where you mean.
Lennie Can you show me?
Baskerville (*slowly*) I know a secret way.
Lennie Good. But I must rest first. (*He lies on the rock*)

Baskerville lies down at his feet, on the ground, and sleeps too. The Lights fade to black

SCENE 13

Over the Edge—Slipping Away

Music: Orion and Cassiopeia theme

Lights: top stage, blue gels; lower stage, c spot, low, on Lennie and Baskerville

Orion and Cassiopeia enter

Orion I'm really worried.
Cassiopeia About the children?
Orion Yes, I can feel our powers draining away, the connection with the world Under the Edge is weakening. Millie, Lennie and Em may all be lost down there. We might never see them again.
Cassiopeia Orion, we must be positive for them. Lennie is strong and has been since he was born. He will find a way out of this for all of them. We must have faith in the children. They won't let us down.
Orion You're right, we must send out good thoughts for Lennie.

The Lights on the top stage fade, c spot comes up on Lennie

Lennie (*sitting up slowly, determined*) Yes, my parents' thoughts are with me. I will go on.

Lennie wakes Baskerville and they exit us front, through the audience

The Lights fade to black

SCENE 14

Under the Edge—The Rescue Concluded

Music: suspense, in background throughout rescue; then audience participation; then Clean-Up Dance—possibly African/South American, with a strong 4/4 beat

Lights: top stage, dark; lower stage, moonlight, searchlights moving around throughout

Farmers downstage (sitting, helmeted—zonked) Pete, Charley, Millie, Em DS (two on either side of the C block—also helmeted and zonked). Bob, Mack and Bullies sitting facing DS on C block. Dancers/Robots kneeling, heads down, facing US

Baskerville and Lennie enter, creeping on from the UC entrance, beyond the audience

They look around and move very slowly, pausing after taking each few steps. When they move on to the lower stage area, they trigger an alarm—a cast member makes a loud alarm sound, OS

Bob *(shouting)* The alarm. Activate the defence robots.
Mack Robots activated!

Cast members make steady beats of drum, off. After 4 beats the robots stir. Each head comes up in turn. (The number of beats is equal to the number of robots)

> *Right fist up, left fist up, right knee, stand (4 beats)*
> *Right arm out, left arm out, right palm up, left palm up (4 beats)*
> *Right leg forward, left, right, left, right, left, right, legs together (8 beats)*

While this is happening Lennie and Baskerville are terrified. Lennie desperately tries to remember the password for the earthquake

The robots stop

Lennie *(shouting)* Shake!

The audience makes its earthquake sounds. The robots are shaken to the ground

Bob (*shouting*) They've stopped the robots. Quick, the security door.
Mack Door activated!

Cast members form a door, several children thick, in front of the Bullies and Bob and Mack. Searchlights increase speed. Lennie and Baskerville are ducking to avoid them

Lennie We'll never make it through with these searchlights. I'll try to get rid of them. Oh no, what was that other word? (*Suddenly he remembers*) Storm!

The audience makes its storm sounds. The searchlights flicker and then go out, leaving the moonlight shining. Lennie and Baskerville creep towards the security door. Lennie points at it

Flash!

As section c delivers the lightning flash (with simultaneous thunder clap), the door falls open and the villains are temporarily stunned. Lennie and Baskerville go through the collapsed doors. The lower stage Lights come up. Lennie finds the main power source

If only I can break this. (*He holds up a lead*) Quick, Baskerville, you can bite through it.

Baskerville does as he is told

Now let's free my sisters and our friends.

Baskerville and Lennie remove the four helmets. The Bullies and Bob and Mack begin to stir

Bob What's happening?

Lennie puts a helmet on him, and one on Mack; Baskerville puts two on the Bullies

Lennie Oh, no, you don't.

Lennie and Baskerville bring Millie, Charley, Em and Pete forward and are happily reunited. Lennie introduces Baskerville to them

Charley Let's free the poor old farmers.
Millie Yes, I'll help.

They bring forward the Farmers in turn. As they are released the Farmers each make a comment

Farmer 1 I'm free.
Farmer 2 I need to get out in the fresh air.
Farmer 3 I've got a terrible headache.
Farmer 4 I had such a strange dream.
Farmer 5 I think I've been in another dimension.

The children all sit down

Lennie I think I can hear something.

Squeaks, bubbling, miaowing are heard from off stage

It's the animals, they've come out of hiding.

The animals enter and cuddle up to the children

The cat miaows to Lennie

They've made us sandwiches too!

They all laugh

Pete I think we could alter the computer and use it to make the robots and villains clean up all the mess they've made. (*He goes over to do this*)

Music for the Clean-up Dance starts. Robots, door guards, Bullies and Bob and Mack get up slowly, shake themselves and pass imaginary brooms and dusters etc. along to each other

Dance: (2 capable dancers could face the others, to give a lead)

> *Shuffle steps forwards, sweeping with a broom (4 beats)*
> *Left/right steps backwards, dropping litter in a bag (4 beats)*
> *Small steps forwards, pressing polish spray twice with left hand, wiping cloth twice with right hand, hand movements repeated on completion (4 beats)*
> *Larger steps backwards, waving arms, alternately, like dusters (4 beats)*

This sequence is repeated as groups of performers join in, so that eventually the whole cast is dancing. When they are all there, the front group leads them all out of the hall, still dancing

SCENE 15

Under and Over the Edge—Finale

Lights: top stage, blue gels and moonlight; lower stage, warm reds and spotlights

Perry and Dawes enter

They explain to the audience that, thanks to their help, all is now well Under and Over the Edge. They announce that a concert will now be held to celebrate the restoration of order and the strengthened link between the two worlds

Orion and Cassiopeia are introduced as the guests of honour

Perry and Dawes introduce the cast (their character names). In turn they perform to each other—songs, dances, jokes, magic acts (each one fairly brief). This is a chance for children who have not had major parts to do a performance. Orchestra and backstage are thanked, and everyone goes off to applause

Finally, Chaos briefly appears in a red spotlight (reminding us of danger still present), and a poem about the future and optimism is read off. (The original production used The Trees *by Philip Larkin for which permission should be sought; or the children could write their own piece)*

CURTAIN

FURNITURE AND PROPERTY LIST

Further dressing may be added at the director's discretion

PROLOGUE

On stage: Stage block(s)

SCENE 1

On stage: As before

Off stage: Large flower (**Orion**)
Large flower (**Cassiopeia**)

Personal: **Perry:** long piece of paper

SCENE 2

On stage: 4 fairground booths

Off stage: Tin whistle or recorder, large round basket, lizard puppet
(**Snake Charmer**)

Personal: **Pete:** money
Charley: money

SCENE 3

Strike: Fairground booths

Off stage: Cymbals, flexible board, drums (**Children**)

SCENE 4

On stage: Pile of wood

Off stage: "rain-maker" tubes (**Children**)
Long blue material (**Children**)

SCENE 5

On stage: 3 bars
Chairs
Glasses
Beer mats
Clothes
Cloth
Food
Covered pub name banner
Darts
Dominoes

Off stage: Clipboard, pen (**Bob**)
Clipboard, pen (**Mack**)

SCENE 6

Strike: Bars

Personal: **Children:** sweets

SCENE 7

On stage: As before

SCENE 8

On stage: As before

Off stage: Helmets (**Bob** and **Mack**)
Heavy black/silver/grey plastic sheets, metal and hard
plastic pipes (**Machines**)

Personal: **Farmer:** money

SCENE 9

On stage: Rock
Machines with levers
Microphone (optional)

SCENE 10

On stage: As before

Personal: **Bob:** wads of notes
Mack: wads of notes

SCENE 11

On stage: As before

Off stage: Bag/box of percussion instruments, lightning flash prop
(**Perry** and **Dawes**)

SCENE 12

On stage: As before

SCENE 13

On stage: As before

SCENE 14

On stage: As before

Personal: **Farmers:** helmets
Children: helmets

SCENE 15

On stage: As before

LIGHTING PLOT

Property fittings required: nil
Various interior and exterior settings

Prologue

To open: Top and lower stages dark

No cues

Scene 1

To open: Top stage, blue gels, pool of moonlight; lower stage, dark; house
             lights, down

No cues

Scene 2

To open: Top stage, blue gels; lower stage, bright with spot c; house lights,
             down

Cue 1   **People** enter   (Page 4)
          Focus spotlight on each stall as script page 4

Scene 3

To open: Top stage, blue flashes of lightning; lower stage, red storm lightning

No cues

SCENE 4

To open: Top stage, occasional blue flashes of lightning; lower stage, red/blue glow

No cues

SCENE 5

To open: Top stage, dark; lower stage, bright interior

No cues

SCENE 6

To open: Top stage, dark; lower stage, bright exterior

No cues

SCENE 7

To open: Top stage, warm yellow, pools of light; lower stage, dark, but with **Millie** and **Lennie** visible

No cues

SCENE 8

To open: Top stage, dark; lower stage, harsh and bright

No cues

SCENE 9

To open: Top stage, dark; lower stage, dim

Cue 2 **Mack** switches off lights   (Page 19)
         Fade lights to semi-darkness

Cue 3   **Bob** springs trap   (Page 19)
              Bring up lights

Cue 4   **All** freeze   (Page 19)
              Black-out

Cue 5   **Lennie** enters   (Page 19)
              Follow spot on **Lennie**

Scene 10

To open: Top stage, dark; lower stage, interior, night, spooky

Cue 6   **Chaos** appears on top stage   (Page 20)
              Red spotlight on **Chaos**

Cue 7   **Chaos** exits   (Page 21)
              Fade lights to dark

Cue 8   **Bob**: "…we must finish his work."   (Page 21)
              Black-out

Scene 11

To open: Top stage, dark; lower stage, interior, bright; house lights, up

No cues

Scene 12

To open: Top stage, dark; lower stage, c spot on **Lennie**, moonlight, and follow
              spot

Cue 9   **Baskerville** sleeps   (Page 24)
              Fade lights to black

Scene 13

To open: Top stage, blue gels; lower stage, c spot, low, on **Lennie** and
              Baskerville

Cue 10   **Orion**: "…good thoughts for Lennie."   (Page 24)
                  Fade lights on top stage, bring up spot C *on* **Lennie**

Cue 11   **Lennie** and **Baskerville** exit   (Page 24)
                  Fade lights to black

SCENE 14

To open: Top stage, dark; lower stage, moonlight, searchlights moving around
                  throughout

Cue 12   **Cast members** form a door   (Page 26)
                  Increase speed of searchlights

Cue 13   **Audience** makes storm sounds.   (Page 26)
                  Flicker searchlights, then cut, leaving moonlight effect

Cue 14   **Lennie** goes through collapsed doors   (Page 26)
                  Bring up lower stage lights

SCENE 15

To open: Top stage, blue gels and moonlight; lower stage, warm reds and
                  spotlights

Cue 15   **Everyone** goes off to applause   (Page 28)
                  Red spotlight on **Chaos**

EFFECTS PLOT

MADE AND PRINTED IN GREAT BRITAIN BY
LATIMER TREND & COMPANY LTD PLYMOUTH
MADE IN ENGLAND